Indignez-vous! Part II, Time for Outrage

Dalek Iga Ghandi

authorHOUSE®

AuthorHouse™ LLC
1663 Liberty Drive
Bloomington, IN 47403
www.authorhouse.com
Phone: 1-800-839-8640

Published by AuthorHouse   07/31/2014

ISBN: 978-1-4969-3096-5 (sc)
ISBN: 978-1-4969-3095-8 (e)

CONTENTS

INTRODUCTION:

Forty two years old. In the middle of the last leg of my journey. I am lucky to have experienced many journeys and hear about the experiences of others. I have a passion for standing up for the downtrodden and the oppressed. If there are two parties and I do not know much about them, my inclination is to support the underdog.

I was inspired by Stephane Hessel when I picked up his little red book. I could not put it down until I read each and every word. Short, to the point and enlightening, were a few words that came to my mind. To do a follow-up on a book that is of such high esteem, is quite a task. But necessity demands an encore. In light of the recent economic upheavals, I felt compelled to carry on the work of Stephane and inspire the next generation to carry on the torch that he lit. Will I be successful in bringing about revolution that will make this a better World as envisioned by Stephane? The number of books in paper or electronic format that will be sold will not determine that. But rather, it will be from actual measurable change and that will determine the success of this book and the previous work by Stephane. I hope my readers will be inspired to carry on the torch that was once lit by the great indomitable spirit of Stephane Hessel.

I owe a debt of gratitude to the fruit seller who sacrificed his own life to start the Arab Spring. I also owe a debt of gratitude to Georgiy Gondadze who gave up his life and allowed the Orange Revolution to take place. Unlike my predecessor, who wrote the first version of Time for Outrage, I will not go into details of my life or experiences. This book was intentionally written using a pseudonym. Part of the reason is because as a person, I don't enjoy the limelight, but rather enjoy seeing the fruits of a vision come true. Another reason for my anonymity is the highly charged atmosphere in my country, where speaking out is often considered unpatriotic, rather than a benefit to the democratic process.

I write this book to continue on the tradition of Occupy Wall Street. The movement touched on some very important ideas of how the 1% of society controls majority of the wealth. This book will focus on how a true revolution will make people aware of the root causes of inequity. I hope to touch on a few methods by which readers of this book will be inspired to take action.

CHAPTER: THE CAUSES OF ILLNESS

The Global financial system was brought to its knees after the housing bubble crash of 2008. One of the lessons learned is the fragile and interconnected nature of the whole system. Another important lesson learned is that assets, cash and equity are somewhat unimportant without the citizens who work hard to maintain the financial apparatus. The proof of this is evident if one investigates the measures taken by lending institutions for every nation that was on the verge of collapse. Each nation tightened its belt and allowed for employment opportunities for those without jobs. Without people working and depositing funds in bank accounts, buying and selling stocks, being avid consumers, the modern financial system stands little chance to survive.

So readers of the book should understand that despite being in the lower totem pole of decision making, we wield quite a bit of power. This power can be delivered if people understand that the fundamental cause of inflation and stagnating economies is the enormous debts that nations pile up. To pay back this debt, poor and rich countries alike have to raise taxes and require its workforce to accept less than acceptable benefits as a citizen of a connected World. The fundamental cause of the rising illness is the great amount of debt countries are taking on to fend off one financial crisis after another.

CHAPTER: A VIABLE PLAN

I propose that world citizenry should analyze the current situation to come up with a viable plan of action to tackle the root causes of the problem. Parliaments and senates of countries will not pass legislation voiding the enormous debt they owe to lending institutions. These financial institutions have become part and parcel of each respective country. Often they control the global scene in the guise of G8, Central Bank of X, the IMF or the World Bank. The influence wielded by these institutions reaches the farthest corners of the globe. To tackle this problem, the citizens of the World would have to take the system down like a chain of dominoes. They have to first come to the realization that in order make a living, put money away for savings and enjoy a decent lifestyle, they need a vibrant economy. Preferably this economy is free from the shackles of the current system - enslavement to a growing debt. The net result of governments being in debt is having a middle class by name only and enslavement of the people. In some third world countries, the debt to income ratio is so high that revolution should be the only means to free the people.

CHAPTER: ONE BODY MANY SOULS:

This chapter is dedicated to the idea that we cannot achieve victory until we decide that victory has to be achieved by each and every people on Earth, every nation and every continent. Then and only then we will call it victory. The pains of the uninsured 'middle class' American who can barely afford health insurance but cannot afford dental care, must be felt by the European who would have a difficult time to fathom this concept. The pains of the Indian farmer who has lost his family farm, has to be felt by the Brazilian student who is going fresh out of college in to the world of finance – in debt 'up to his/her eyeballs'. The struggle of the 6 million plus prisoners in the American Industrial-Prison Complex has to be dealt with by a world body if the country itself does not have the temerity to deal with this issue. The racial injustices in India's underclass is similar to the African American struggle in the US, even after election of an African American President. Socialists agenda's of taxing the rich to 75% tax rate or conservative agendas of eliminating social programs is not the answer. The true answer lies somewhere in the middle. As a single body, we must find answers to distribute newly invented drugs to the whole World and understand that one system of pricing will not allow every single country to benefit from the drug. Under the current model, many countries in Africa and Asia go in to enormous amounts of debt, just to purchase drugs from Western nations. A two fold approach may solve the problem. First and foremost, the idea that research and development of newly formed drugs can only be accomplished through a 'for profit model' has to be explored. Lessons learned is the fact the expenditure of dollars does not translate into better healthcare. Clearly some European countries have the lead when it comes to having healthcare systems that work to benefit the overall population. A hybrid system of healthcare has to be created based on economy and specific health needs of the people.

A few core ideals have to established that I believe will assist in setting up or modifying existing systems of healthcare:

- Healthcare model must offer healthcare to any citizen or non-citizen without scrutinizing their identity
- Healthcare must include complete care, including mental health and dental health
- Medicine should be encouraged to practice for those who like healing and dealing with people rather than a group of individuals

who feel that is one of the best professions to earn a great deal of money
- A world body has to be created to inform each and every nation to return to better forms of nutrition and exercise

We cannot have food police to take away the rights of the people to choose the kinds of food or the lifestyle they choose. But, we can at least inform and let the citizens of each nation decide.

CHAPTER: REVOLUTION

What kind of revolution am I envisioning? I believe we should learn from our success stories. The Arab Spring and the Orange Revolution were extremely successful for the most part. I envision the citizens of the world will use social media to choose a single country where the chances of success of a citizen lead revolution is very high. In the first phase of this revolution, the people in a few countries will rise up and stop all financial centers from functioning. This should continue until the elected governments void all the past interest based contracts owned by their respective governments. Then the people should find means to create banks that will allow governments to print money without borrowing with interest. If governments themselves can print money at will, why should they allow private institutions to charge a high rate of interest? The elite and ruling classes of the respective countries are not paying a price. They get a large incentive for being colluders with the banking and lending class. As a result, they could care less if the people of these indebted countries have to forgo their pension plans, work two or three jobs or take out retirement altogether from their life plans.

The plan to free the World from the invisible slavery entails some brave and technologically savvy souls to develop applications for the current crop of mobile devices. These applications should allow a group gathered in vicinity to share their Internet connections. This will allow groups in the area to communicate even if governments decide to shut down parts of the Internet or a particular cell tower.

Choosing the country that will lead the charge is a bit more difficult. My personal choice would be a South American country. The fervor of revolution is quite high in many of these countries due to a highly educated younger generation who are tired of the status quo.

PALESTINE

The past author had a chapter on the Israeli Palestinian conflict. My first draft of this book had very few words compared to Stephen, in regards to Palestine. Part of the reason, is that I am not Jewish and Stephen was in a better position to criticize Zionist Jews, than me. But as I am hearing about stories of Israeli atrocities in the last days of July, 2014, I share the outrage that Stephen felt when he was observing the conflict. The scale of the current atrocities is probably on a scale, higher by a few magnitudes, than in the past. Is the World watching? Yes, but silently and with the resilience to slap Israel's arms with a Security Council Resolution that may or may not come out over the objection of its closest ally. War crimes, genocide and deliberate targeting of the innocent, are a few words that are going around the circle of people who seem to care. Suffice it to suggest that it would be in the best interest of the Israeli people to allow their Palestinian brethren to have a free and fully sovereign state. Let Israel be aware that the forces that created Salahdin to invade Palestine and free it from tyrants of a different kind, are brewing in and around its borders. The dispersed Kurds are gaining some autonomy from the scars left by the divisions of the Colonial demarcations and scheming. Not afar, the Islamic World has witnessed the creation of the first "Khalifate." Whether or not these ventures will be successful will be matter of time. But a new generation of Islamic fighters rising from the ashes of conflicts in Syria, Afghanistan and Iraq are hymning the poetry of returning the freedom of Palestine. So, let the wise and those with conscience among the Israelis, its diaspora and those who care deeply about its future, understand this: Electing right wing governments is not the solution to Israeli problems. Israel needs bold leaders like Rabin to forge a real peace and accept the 1967 borders, period. The future of the Israelis living in these borrowed lands depends on it. A quick browsing of history will illuminate the fact that the first state that was chosen as a homeland for the Israeli diaspora was not Palestine, but rather Uganda. Uganda, a land where I have much connection.

Suggested reading for those who care and would like to learn more about the Israeli aggression conflict can be found be reading the Goldstone Report of 2009 as Stephen suggested. But, I would rather direct the readers to the history of the land and suggest that they read the history of each successive rulers in the land for the past 1000 years. They will find that after each massacre and genocide, the World, even without much technology or news in existence today, rallied and managed to drive succeeding generations of war criminals out of Palestine. Let this be a warning to the Israeli army and those in power that the World is observing. Your war crimes will be punished using the same methods that were developed in Nuremberg. If you truly believe in your scripture then the fear of God should prevent you from doing the ghastly deeds and face the cameras with the same sickening smile as that of Milosevic and Mladic. Let the Jews of Israel be aware of Zechariah 9:9, and it's fulfillment for the third and final time.

CHAPTER: TIME OUT, TYRANTS!

Time is running out for tyrants and usurpers of power throughout the world. I can sense that a generation of users are growing up on social media, electronic devices and video games. These are used for the purpose of instant gratification. These tools can also be used as a power of good. The young generation can take this habit of not waiting for change and can make change happen with a few clicks on their iPhones or Android devices.

CHAPTER: NON VIOLENCE, THE ONLY WAY:

I wanted to devote a chapter to emphasize how important it is for this movement to remain non-violent. Unlike my predecessor, I am not convinced that non-violence should completely be taken out of the picture. The age of Martin Luther King, Ghandi and Nelson Mandela remain relevant as it ever was. The power of violence should not be underestimated; however, there is no room for violence in this movement.

For this particular movement to be successful it should focus all its energy to ensure that each and every individual remain non-violent. In this age of spying and technologies, I will assume that a great number of the participants maybe government informants or part of law enforcement. I would like to remind that the movement's ideals are based on equity and justice. As such, participants should not try to weed out informants among each other.

Rather, the focus should be to carry out the mission of freeing a city, a county and a country, until the whole World has rid itself from the shackles and chains that holds its population from reaching a blissful co-existence.

CHAPTER: SLAVERY EXISTS!

The shackles of slavery and the system of indentured servants have vanished from most parts of the world. But a new invisible shackle in the guise of high interest rates is imprisoning our hopes and dreams for the future. If we were to color code the countries of the World with blue being severely indebted middle income countries, red being severely indebted low-income countries, while yellow is moderately indebted low-income countries we would see an alarming pattern. We would find that most of Africa is red with a few exceptions to the North and South. We would find that most of South America is Blue with exception of a few countries in the North. We do not have to accept a future where our old are required to keep on working. Our future should not be devoid of acceptable health care. It should not be devoid of families enjoying a meal at the end of the day. Rather under today's circumstances, the father and the mother are both working additional hours to make ends meet. The high burden from interest rates is flowing down the path of each and every family and young student. A student of any discipline in many developed nation is burdened with enormous debts after graduation. Can we as a society, not allow our young to graduate without debt? Often this debt is so enormous, that the person has to work half their lives, to pay it off. Each person in the Third World owes about $500 to the West. Africa spends 4 times as much on repaying it's debt than it does on healthcare. The income inequality that Stephane mentioned in his work is far greater today than when he wrote and published his book. Today the 20 percent of the World's poorest are dwarfed by the 20 percent of the richest by a factor of 60.

It is beyond the scope of this book to tackle issues of high utility fees and increase of basic housing. The readers of this book are intelligent enough to understand when the high cost of living becomes an epidemic and new movements and revolutions are necessary. I want to focus on eradicating the shackle that is put on countries due to the current system of finances of printing or borrowing money. The readers should also be aware that often large loans made by IMF or the World Bank are not beneficial in the long term, for the people of the respective countries that it is meant to help. These large loans often benefit a few people at the top of the food chain in these countries. There is a trickledown effect, but it may be so tiny in terms of trickling down, that it is better for the recipients of these loans to just say, "No Thank you."

CHAPTER: ENERGY, THE ISSUE THAT MUST BE SOLVED:

Other issue that the next generation has to tackle is the issue of energy. Can we live in a World where we are not destroying the Earth in search of new forms of fossil fuel? What about the mutilated Earth from creation of dams that are blocking rivers and waterways? Yes, the energy received from these water projects is immensely beneficial. What is the net return, we must ask? It is often at the expense of farmers who can no longer farm in a country a few miles down the river where it was dammed. Is nuclear energy the solution? It is beyond the scope of this book to discuss these topics. But the reader should be aware of these issues and put on their thinking caps. Perhaps one of the readers of this book will have a solution that they will share with the World, after being inspired. This chapter is meant to inspire new aspirations and visions to the young and the old alike. So be inspired and dream lots of idealistic dreams!

CHAPTER: PERMACULTURE AND SUSTAINABLE COMMERCIAL AGRICULTURE

The current model of Agriculture based on output of all-out amount of crops for maximum profit, during a corporate reporting period is not a sustainable model. Small scale agriculture and Permaculture based models have to be investigated as human populations continue to increase. Australia has taken some giants steps in regards to Permaculture. We must learn from countries that have had success stories and implement modified versions of the same successful concepts in different parts of the world. What has worked in Vietnam may not work in the deserts of Saudi Arabia. However, the core ideal has to be accepted, i.e., the current model for maximum profit is not sustainable, period. Before embarking on writing this book, I tried my utter best to learn Permaculture principles from a farmer I knew. But, because of distance from my home and other obligations this farmer had, I never managed to apply principles of Permaculture on a real farm. I found the twelve principles of Permaculture as listed by David Holmgren invaluable. As such, I will list them in this chapter. These principles can be applied not only to Permaculture, but other similar issues faced by the reader of this book.

Twelve Permaculture design principles articulated by David Holmgren in his *Permaculture based work is listed below:*

Principles and Pathways Beyond Sustainability

Observe and interact: By taking time to engage with nature we can design solutions that suit our particular situation.

Catch and store energy: By developing systems that collect resources at peak abundance, we can use them in times of need.

Obtain a yield: Ensure that you are getting truly useful rewards as part of the work that you are doing.

Apply self-regulation and accept feedback: We need to discourage inappropriate activity to ensure that systems can continue to function well.

Use and value renewable *resources and services*: Make the best use of nature's abundance to reduce our consumptive behavior and dependence on non-renewable resources.

Produce no waste: By valuing and making use of all the resources that are available to us, nothing goes to waste.

Design from patterns to details: By stepping back, we can observe patterns in nature and society. These can form the backbone of our designs, with the details filled in as we go.

Integrate rather than segregate: By putting the right things in the right place, relationships develop between those things and they work together to support each other.

Use small and slow solutions: Small and slow systems are easier to maintain than big ones, making better use of local resources and producing more sustainable outcomes.

Use and value diversity: Diversity reduces vulnerability to a variety of threats and takes advantage of the unique nature of the environment in which it resides.

Use edges and value the marginal: The interface between things is where the most interesting events take place. These are often the most valuable, diverse and productive elements in the system.

Creatively use and respond to change: We can have a positive impact on inevitable change by carefully observing, and then intervening at the right time.

A good deal of the resources of our nations have to be invested in Mycology or the study of fungi, with the intent to benefit from them. Enough investment in it may yield for us new types of drugs and food sources. It may teach us a lesson or two about recycling waste including those we think are toxic beyond the point of return. Solutions such as the use of Water Hyacinth to clean polluted rivers or use intelligent agricultural techniques to desalinate agriculture fields have to be explored. Funding reserved for defense or ostentatious projects, that serve little purpose other than to build politician's resumes can and should be used for these research funds. I urge the reader of this book to rise up to the challenge and start acting and thinking like a revolutionary. Revolutionaries can effect change and make lasting impacts. It has to be balanced with planning, patience and perseverance.

CHAPTER: NUCLEAR ENERGY

I wanted to devote an entire chapter to the topic of acquiring our energy from a mixture of sustainable forms of energy, including Nuclear Energy. Before Nuclear as an energy option can be discussed, I wanted to bring the reader's attention to the number of accidents that have occurred over the years in regards to Nuclear weapons and peaceful Nuclear reactors. The close calls that have been recorded in the annals of history have proven one simple fact - Nuclear Weapons are not acceptable, period.

In 1961, in the skies over North Carolina, In the United States, two Hydrogen bombs were dropped after a B-52 bomber was incapacitated. Declassified reports have established that one of the bombs was in the 'armed' setting during the time it hit the ground. The crash actually caused damage to the switch contacts which prevented a denotation of the most dangerous weapon known to mankind. The other bomb went through all the stages of detonation before a failure to detonate, saved the people of North Carolina. God's handiwork? Perhaps!

A similar accident took place over the skies of New Mexico in the United States on May 22nd, 1957. A 12 feet by 25 feet crater was created when a B-36 aircraft carrying a nuclear bomb dropped it in midair. Luckily the nuclear capsule separated and the New Mexicans were averted from disaster.

On February 5th, 1958, a B-57 carrying a nuclear bomb collided with an F-86. The Nuclear device was never located.

On March 14th, 1961 in Yuba City, California, a B-52 carrying a pair of nuclear weapons suffered pressure loss at 10,000 feet. The bombs were subsequently recovered but a disaster was seconds away.

On January 17th, 1966, In Palomares, Spain, a B-52 carrying four hydrogen bombs exploded. The irony in this case was that a total disaster was prevented because of a low voltage switch, which failed to function.

According to a researcher named Schlosser, about 700 accidents involving United States nuclear arsenals occurred between 1950 and 1968.

A significant mention would be near launching of a nuclear weapon during the Clinton Administration over the European skies.

These near misses itself, speaks volumes to us that 'near misses' are not acceptable when it comes to nuclear weapons or usage of nuclear reactors for civilian benefit. We must use our ability to innovate as a race to come up with safer solutions for nuclear fuel as a viable energy option. We have to ask ourselves questions such as, is it feasible in the near future, to store tons of nuclear waste in the craters of the Moon or in orbits around the Sun? Is it possible for the new generation of smart engineers to focus their attention from building a more powerful nuclear bomb, to building a nuclear reactor that will not remind us of a Fukushima or a Love Canal? I truly believe that 'safe nuclear energy' is within our reach. But research and development dollars are being diverted to the wrong projects because of lack of guidance and rejection of priorities based on acceptance of 'a deviant moral code'.

CHAPTER: %1 INSPIRATION:

This chapter was inspired by the infamous Thomas Edison quote that genius is "1% Inspiration and 99% perspiration." As a man of God, with a firm ground of my religion, I wanted to write a book that does not force the reader to be inspired by sources of faith. A reader should keep in mind that every movement needs a soul for it to be successful. If the reader is comfortable with a particular religious source for guidance, after a long day of revolutionary activities, then they should seek solace in that. After studying many sources, I recommend the readers of this book who are of lesser religious inclination to be inspired by the writings of Paul Coelho[1]. I will use a short quote from his book, The Warrior of Light. Mr. Coelho writes, "A Warrior of Light does not waste his time listening to provocations; he has a destiny to fulfill." Another book that I draw inspiration from on a regular basis is, Zen In The Martial Arts. This book is concise, to the point, but beneficial in assisting the tired revolutionary at the end of an arduous day. A revolution takes courage and inner strength. All of this can be accumulated from diving into inspirations from the past and the present. Whatever inspires you to continue on the path with abiding resilience is what you should be inspired by. It may the Batman Comic Strips or a book of poetry written by your late grandfather. Be inspired, do good deeds and continue to effect lasting change.

CHAPTER: TIMING

Timing is as important as it ever was. **September 17th** is an excellent date to kick-off this revolution. Let us start with informing and educating those who want to participate. Education is the key to power. The revolutionaries must not rise up until each and everyone has an understanding of what it is that they are fighting for. As part of the movement, we have to change our attitudes from being a consumer class to a more spiritual being. Is our main goal in life to earn a living and spend most of what we earn on a series of movies, gadgets and video games? As a society we must put more emphasis on human to human interaction and love and bond with each member of our close family.

Perhaps some societies where the 18 year old is asked to move out will have to let their young child stay a bit longer. Let them save and get a good education or learn a valuable skill before trying to stand on their own feet. Let us dream as revolutionaries dream and take advantage of this new social media spurned on by the age of Internet. Let us share our dreams and aspirations using this newly discovered tool to rid ourselves of our vices. Big dreams are achievable. We only need a few who are dedicated, educated and enlightened with the wisdom to understand that the status quo is not an option.

ACKNOWLEDGEMENTS:

The inspirations for this book came from many sources. My family, friends and acquaintances had some role in formulating my ideas. My wife has been a constant source of inspiration and encouragement. She has often been the source of educating me on documentaries such as Dirty Wars or a paradigm shifting piece by Spurlock. One person in particular is a mother of two, whose every word inspired me to create some chapters in this book, particularly the ones on Permaculture and sustainable living. She along with her friends has been vocal with the Facebook #Red Out Campaign. As a man of history, I am coming to the conclusion reached by Malcolm X, i.e., a man should resort to non-violent means to achieve a given objective. There will be cases where you will face an adversary who understands nothing, except the power of the unsheathed sword. The other inspirations came from watching the media display injustices and sufferings of the Palestinian people or the Rohinga people in present day

Myanmar. Some sufferings are clearly visible on the television screens while others like the tooth ache of a working mother (or an university student in an 'affluent academy – in a developed nation) who cannot afford dental care, is something that will go unnoticed by census work and statistics alike. Only a group of human beings with empathy can discover the problem and find a solution to it. In a sense, it is the lack of empathy in the coming generation that inspired me to write. Is the new generation incapable of empathy? On the contrary, I believe they can be better than past generations when it comes to understanding the core concepts, i.e., human beings are one body with many souls, regardless of our social standings or the countries that we live in. I believe this concept is more evident to the new generation because of existence of social media that has been the purveyor of all things, good or bad. Should you start burning your passports as you read this book and apply to become a "Citizen of the World?" Not yet, but hold on to your dreams. They will be answered completely and beyond your wildest imagination. So imagine, hold steadfast and inspire!

ENDNOTES

1. The inspiration for using Paul Coelho came from the same mother of two referenced in the end of the book.

ABOUT THE AUTHOR

Born exactly 10 years after the prophesized birth of the Anti-Christ, as foretold by a famous Christian astrologer, the author did not find any mark of the beast on the back of his head. Rather, than discovering '666', what he came across was a growing bald spot. He was born in what he proudly calls, "The capital of the poorest country in the World" (though in reality, it is not in that category, according to most statistics). At the age of four, he left his birthplace and moved with his family to Kampala, Uganda. There, his younger brother was born, under the government of Edi Amin. The author's family left Uganda and moved to Jeddah Saudi Arabia, for the next four years. He was not a fan of the moral decay in Saudi culture, despite an outward appearance of piety. He was quite content to move to Los Angeles and continue his middle school education in the public schools of Los Angeles. During his time in Los Angeles, his family was homeless for a few months due to rancor among his parents, who subsequently divorced.

He remembers his time living in Hollywood, on top of a XXX theater and walking down Hollywood Boulevard, admiring the names of famous stars. His family would often travel to the farms of Bakersfield working on grape fields.

In the subsequent months, after a short stay in Fresno, California, his family made the permanent move to Bakersfield, where he completed his sophomore and junior year in high school. During this time, he devoted much of his time learning about religions and learning the Martial Arts. Thereafter, his family moved to San Diego, California. He attended University of California San Diego, starting as an Engineering Physics Major. He switched to teaching as a major and subsequently to Bio-Chemistry by the time he was a junior. Additionally, he completed his associates' degree in Japanese and Computer Science while at UCSD. During his five years of college, the author was blessed to have the opportunity to travel around the world and visit countries like India, Australia, Malaysia, Canada and England among many other countries in all continents except Antarctica. During his travels, he came across sages who taught him different disciplines and philosophies. He started a venture into publishing while in college and tried a six month unsuccessful attempt at having his own Martial Arts School in the discipline of Shotokan Karate. After college, he graduated towards becoming an independent computer consultant and founded his consulting farm. References from college landed him a job as a supervisor/manager of technology with a bio-tech firm in San Diego. After two years in the bio-tech world, he resigned from his position to devote his energy to assist a failed dot.com venture. During this period, the author met his wife in Baltimore and subsequently married her in his native San Diego. He moved out of San Diego to the East Coast in 2000. During the next 14 years, he spent much of his time as a Healthcare consultant. He currently resides in the State of Maryland and considers himself as a displaced Californian in the East Coast. The author is working on the third revision of this book among other hobbies such as working on the Unified Theorem that Einstein failed to discover. He is the father of 5 children and looks forward to having more children through adoption or as a foster parent. His greatest love is to look at the face of his children as they are smiling.